D1542679

SUPER BOWL

SAN FRANCISCO 49ERS

CHAMPIONS

SUPER BOWL

Published by Creative Education
123 South Broad Street
Mankato, Minnesota 56001
Creative Education is an imprint of The Creative Company.

DESIGN AND PRODUCTION BY **EVANSDAY DESIGN**

LIBRARY OF CONGRESS CATALOGING-IN-PUBLICATION DATA

LeBoutillier, Nate.
San Francisco 49ers / by Nate LeBoutillier.
p. cm. — (Super Bowl champions)
Includes index.
ISBN 1-58341-391-X
1. San Francisco 49ers (Football team)—Juvenile literature. I. Title. II. Series.
GV956.S3L43 2005
796.332'64'0979461—dc22   2005048360

9 8 7 6 5 4 3 2

COVER PHOTO: tight end Eric Johnson

PHOTOGRAPHS BY

Corbis (Bettmann, Reuters), Getty Images (Lisa Blumenfeld, Bruce Bennett Studios, Otto Greule Jr, Jed Jacbsohn, Doug Pensinger), SportsChrome USA

CHAMPIONS

SAN FRANCISCO 49ERS

THE 49ERS are a professional football team in the National Football League (NFL). They play in San Francisco, California. San Francisco can be a warm place to play football.

THE 49ERS play in a stadium called 3Com Park. Their helmets are gold with the letters "SF" on the side. Their uniforms are gold, red, and beige. The 49ers play many games against teams called the Cardinals, Rams, and Seahawks.

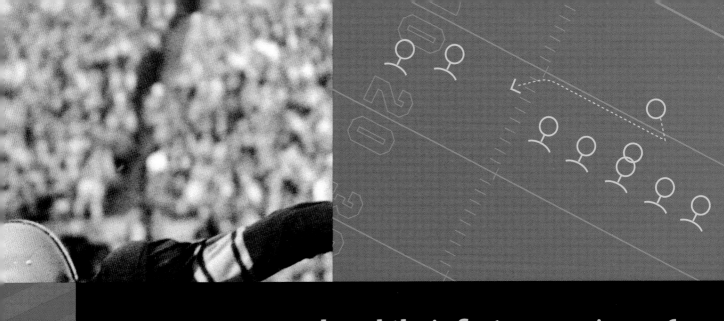

THE 49ERS played their first season in 1946. They were the first professional football team in the western United States. Y.A. Tittle was one of the first great 49ers players. He was a smart quarterback.

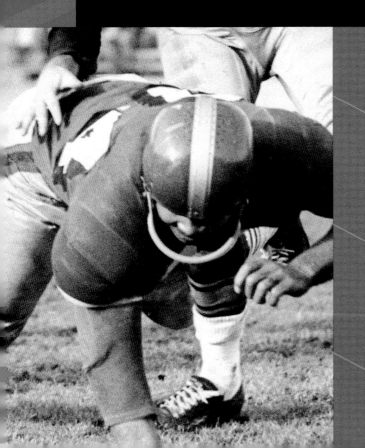

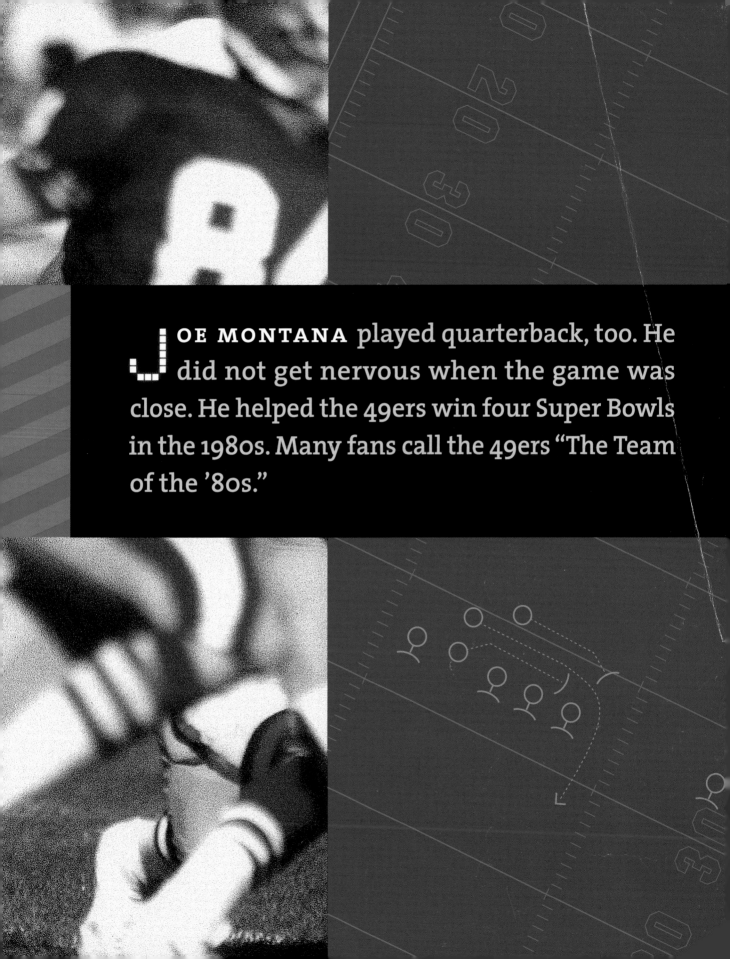

JOE MONTANA played quarterback, too. He did not get nervous when the game was close. He helped the 49ers win four Super Bowls in the 1980s. Many fans call the 49ers "The Team of the '80s."

IN 1981, the 49ers played the Dallas Cowboys in the playoffs. The game was almost over when Joe Montana threw a high pass. Dwight Clark caught it with the tips of his fingers to score a touchdown. The 49ers won by one point! The next game, they won their first Super Bowl.

Dwight Clark's catch in 1981 is a famous play.

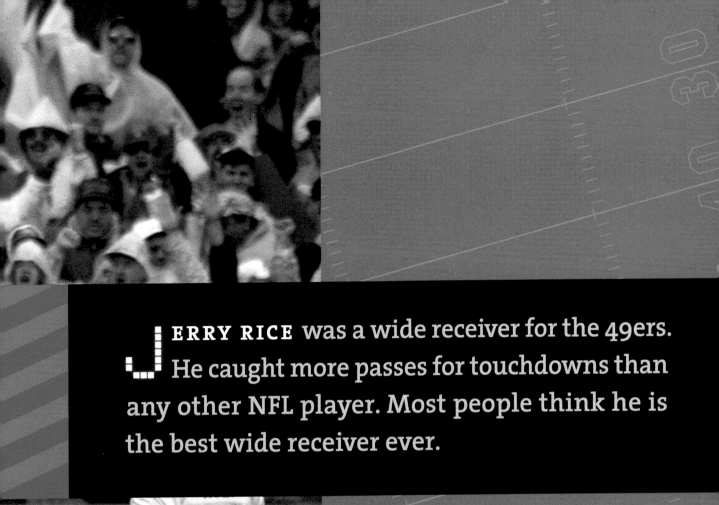

JERRY RICE was a wide receiver for the 49ers. He caught more passes for touchdowns than any other NFL player. Most people think he is the best wide receiver ever.

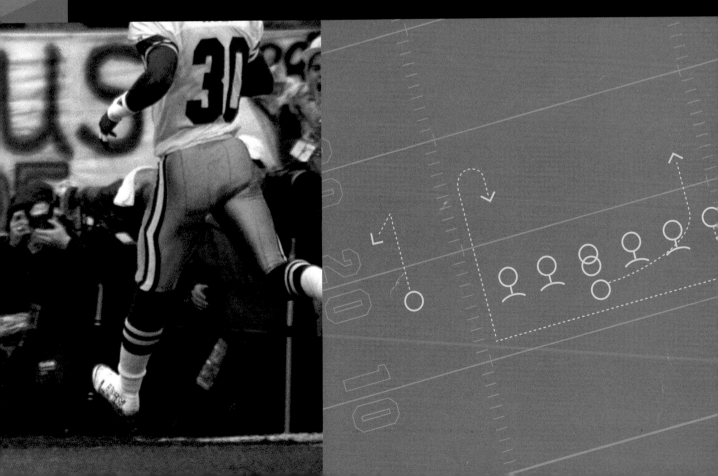

STEVE YOUNG played quarterback after Joe Montana. He was good at passing, but he was also a fast runner. In 1994, he helped the 49ers win the Super Bowl again. He threw six touchdown passes. That is a Super Bowl record.

THE 49ERS have won the Super Bowl five times. No other team has won more than that. The 49ers have never lost in the Super Bowl.

IN 2004, the 49ers won just 2 games and lost 14. Then they hired a new coach named Mike Nolan. 49ers fans hope that he will make the team a champion again!

Today's 49ers players are fighting for another championship

GLOSSARY

National Football League (NFL)

a group of football teams that play against each other;
there are 32 teams in the NFL today

playoffs

games played after a season to see which team is
the best

professional

a person or team that gets paid to play or work

record

something that is the best (or most) ever

Team colors
Gold, red, and beige (yellowish brown)

Home stadium
3Com Park (69,734 seats)

Conference/Division
National Football Conference (NFC), West Division

First season
1946

Super Bowl wins
1981 (beat Cincinnati Bengals 26–21)
1984 (beat Miami Dolphins 38–16)
1988 (beat Cincinnati Bengals 20–16)
1989 (beat Denver Broncos 55–10)
1994 (beat San Diego Chargers 49–26)

Training camp location
Santa Clara, California

NFL Web site for kids
http://www.playfootball.com